Table of Contents

Chapter 1: Understanding Stomach Fat

The Science Behind Stomach Fat

In order to effectively tackle stomach fat, it is crucial to understand the science behind its formation and persistence. Stomach fat, also known as visceral fat, is different from subcutaneous fat which lies just beneath the skin. Visceral fat surrounds vital organs in the abdominal cavity and poses serious health risks such as heart disease, diabetes, and high blood pressure. This type of fat is metabolically active and produces hormones and inflammatory substances that can wreak havoc on the body.

The accumulation of stomach fat is often attributed to a combination of genetics, poor diet, lack of exercise, and hormonal imbalances. When excess calories are consumed and not burned off through physical activity, they are stored as fat in the body, with a tendency for it to accumulate in the abdominal area. Hormones such as cortisol, insulin, and leptin play a role in regulating fat storage and metabolism, and imbalances in these hormones can contribute to stubborn stomach fat.

To effectively target stomach fat, a combination of diet, exercise, and lifestyle changes is essential. High-intensity interval training (HIIT) has been shown to be particularly effective in burning visceral fat due to its ability to increase metabolism and promote fat oxidation. Incorporating strength training exercises that target the core muscles can also help to tone and tighten the abdominal area.

In terms of diet, focusing on whole, nutrient-dense foods such as lean proteins, fruits, vegetables, whole grains, and healthy fats can help to reduce overall body fat and specifically target stomach fat. Avoiding sugary drinks, processed foods, and excessive alcohol consumption is key in preventing the accumulation of visceral fat. Additionally, managing stress levels through techniques such as meditation, yoga, and adequate sleep can help to regulate hormones and reduce belly fat.

Understanding the science behind stomach fat is crucial in developing a targeted approach to losing it quickly and effectively. By incorporating a combination of HIIT workouts, strength training exercises, a healthy diet, and stress management techniques, individuals can see significant reductions in stomach fat and improve their overall health. With dedication and consistency, it is possible to achieve rapid fat loss and achieve a leaner, healthier body.

Why Stomach Fat is Dangerous

Stomach fat, also known as visceral fat, is not just an aesthetic concern. It is actually one of the most dangerous types of fat to have in the body. Unlike subcutaneous fat, which lies just beneath the skin, visceral fat surrounds vital organs such as the liver, pancreas, and intestines. This can lead to a host of health issues, including diabetes, heart disease, and even certain types of cancer. Therefore, it is crucial for those looking to lose weight quickly to focus on reducing stomach fat.

One of the reasons why stomach fat is so dangerous is that it is metabolically active. This means that it releases hormones and other substances that can increase inflammation and insulin resistance in the body. This can lead to a condition known as metabolic syndrome, which is a cluster of conditions that increase the risk of heart disease, stroke, and diabetes. By reducing stomach fat, individuals can improve their overall health and reduce their risk of developing these serious health conditions.

In addition to the health risks associated with stomach fat, it can also have a negative impact on self-esteem and mental health. Many people feel self-conscious about their stomach fat and may avoid social situations or activities that require them to show off their midsection. This can lead to feelings of shame, low self-esteem, and even depression. By shedding stomach fat, individuals can not only improve their physical health but also boost their confidence and sense of well-being.

Furthermore, stomach fat is notoriously stubborn and difficult to get rid of. It often requires a combination of diet, exercise, and lifestyle changes to see significant results. However, with dedication and the right strategies, it is possible to burn stomach fat and achieve a leaner, healthier body. This book will provide readers with the tools and knowledge they need to effectively target and eliminate stomach fat, leading to rapid fat loss and improved overall health.

In conclusion, stomach fat is not just a cosmetic concern – it is a serious health risk that can lead to a range of chronic diseases and negatively impact mental well-being. For those looking to lose weight quickly and effectively, focusing on reducing stomach fat should be a top priority. By following the advice and strategies outlined in this book, readers can take control of their health and achieve their fat loss goals.

Common Causes of Stomach Fat

Stomach fat, also known as visceral fat, is a common concern for many individuals looking to lose weight and improve their overall health. There are several common causes of stomach fat that can contribute to this stubborn area of fat accumulation. One of the main reasons for excess stomach fat is poor diet and nutrition. Consuming a diet high in processed foods, sugar, and unhealthy fats can lead to weight gain, particularly around the midsection.

Additionally, a sedentary lifestyle can also contribute to the accumulation of stomach fat. Lack of physical activity and exercise can slow down metabolism and lead to weight gain, particularly in the abdominal area. It is important to incorporate regular exercise into your routine to help burn calories and reduce stomach fat.

Another common cause of stomach fat is stress. When we are stressed, our bodies release cortisol, a hormone that can lead to fat storage, particularly in the abdominal area. Finding healthy ways to manage stress, such as meditation, yoga, or deep breathing exercises, can help reduce cortisol levels and prevent the accumulation of stomach fat.

Genetics can also play a role in the distribution of fat in the body, including the stomach area. Some individuals may be predisposed to carrying excess weight in their midsection due to their genetic makeup. While genetics cannot be changed, it is still possible to reduce stomach fat through a combination of diet, exercise, and lifestyle changes.

In conclusion, there are several common causes of stomach fat that can contribute to weight gain in this area. By addressing poor diet and nutrition, incorporating regular exercise, managing stress, and understanding the role of genetics, individuals can take steps to reduce stomach fat and improve their overall health. With dedication and commitment, it is possible to achieve rapid fat loss and shed excess weight around the midsection.

Chapter 2: Setting Goals for Rapid Fat Loss

Determining Your Ideal Weight

Determining your ideal weight is an essential step in your journey to rapid fat loss and shredding stomach fat. Your ideal weight is not just a number on the scale, but a reflection of your overall health and well-being. To determine your ideal weight, it is important to consider factors such as your height, age, gender, and body composition. By calculating your ideal weight, you can set realistic goals for your weight loss journey and track your progress effectively.

One of the most common ways to determine your ideal weight is by using the Body Mass Index (BMI) calculator. BMI is a simple tool that calculates your weight in relation to your height and provides a general indication of whether you are underweight, normal weight, overweight, or obese. While BMI is a useful starting point, it is important to remember that it does not take into account factors such as muscle mass and body composition. Therefore, it is important to use BMI as a general guideline rather than a definitive measure of your ideal weight.

Another important factor to consider when determining your ideal weight is your body composition. Body composition refers to the proportion of fat, muscle, and other tissues in your body. A healthy body composition is key to achieving optimal health and fitness. To determine your body composition, you can use tools such as bioelectrical impedance analysis (BIA) scales or skinfold calipers. By assessing your body composition, you can better understand your overall health and set realistic goals for losing stomach fat and achieving your ideal weight.

In addition to BMI and body composition, it is important to consider your individual goals and preferences when determining your ideal weight. Your ideal weight should be a reflection of your personal health and fitness goals, rather than societal standards or unrealistic expectations. By setting realistic and achievable goals for your weight loss journey, you can stay motivated and focused on shredding stomach fat and achieving lasting results. Remember that everyone's ideal weight is different, so it is important to focus on your individual needs and priorities when determining your ideal weight.

In conclusion, determining your ideal weight is a crucial step in your journey to rapid fat loss and shredding stomach fat. By considering factors such as BMI, body composition, and personal goals, you can set realistic expectations for your weight loss journey and track your progress effectively. Remember that your ideal weight is unique to you and should be a reflection of your overall health and well-being. By focusing on your individual needs and priorities, you can achieve lasting results and maintain a healthy lifestyle for years to come.

Creating a Realistic Timeline

Creating a realistic timeline for achieving your fat loss goals is crucial for success. It's important to set realistic expectations and understand that losing stomach fat takes time and dedication. By creating a timeline, you can break down your goals into smaller, manageable steps that will help you stay on track and motivated throughout your fat loss journey.

First and foremost, it's important to set a specific goal for how much stomach fat you want to lose and by when. For example, you might aim to lose 1-2 pounds of stomach fat per week, which is a safe and realistic rate of weight loss. By setting a clear goal, you can create a timeline that outlines the steps you need to take to achieve it, such as following a healthy diet, exercising regularly, and staying consistent with your fat loss efforts.

When creating your timeline, be sure to factor in any obstacles or challenges that may arise along the way. Life can be unpredictable, so it's important to be flexible and adjust your timeline as needed. If you encounter setbacks or plateaus in your fat loss journey, don't get discouraged – instead, reassess your goals and timeline to ensure they are still realistic and achievable.

It's also important to celebrate small victories along the way. Losing stomach fat can be a challenging process, so it's important to acknowledge and celebrate your progress, no matter how small. By setting milestones in your timeline and rewarding yourself for reaching them, you can stay motivated and focused on achieving your ultimate fat loss goals.

In conclusion, creating a realistic timeline for losing stomach fat is essential for success. By setting specific goals, planning out your steps, and staying flexible in the face of obstacles, you can stay on track and motivated throughout your fat loss journey. Remember to celebrate your progress and adjust your timeline as needed to ensure you are on the right track to achieving your ultimate fat loss goals.

Tracking Progress

Tracking your progress is essential when it comes to achieving rapid fat loss, especially in the stomach area. By monitoring your progress, you can see what is working and what may need adjusting in your weight loss journey. One of the best ways to track your progress is by keeping a food journal. Write down everything you eat and drink throughout the day to help you identify any patterns or habits that may be hindering your progress.

In addition to keeping a food journal, it is important to track your physical activity and exercise routines. By keeping a log of your workouts, you can see if you are staying consistent with your exercise regimen and if you need to increase the intensity or duration of your workouts. Tracking your physical activity can also help you identify any plateaus in your weight loss journey so you can make the necessary adjustments to continue seeing results.

Another important aspect of tracking progress is monitoring your measurements. In addition to weighing yourself regularly, it is crucial to measure your waist, hips, and other trouble areas where you may be losing fat. Sometimes the scale may not reflect the changes happening in your body, so taking measurements can give you a more accurate representation of your progress. Seeing inches lost in your waistline can be a great motivator to keep pushing forward with your fat loss goals.

Tracking progress also involves setting specific, measurable, achievable, relevant, and time-bound (SMART) goals. By setting SMART goals, you can create a roadmap for your fat loss journey and have a clear direction of where you want to go. Whether it's losing a certain number of pounds in a month or fitting into a specific pair of jeans, having concrete goals can help keep you focused and motivated throughout your weight loss journey.

In conclusion, tracking your progress is essential for anyone looking to lose stomach fat fast. By keeping a food journal, monitoring your physical activity, tracking your measurements, and setting SMART goals, you can stay on track and make the necessary adjustments to achieve your fat loss goals. Remember that progress may not always be linear, but by staying consistent and committed to your weight loss journey, you can see the results you desire in no time.

Chapter 3: Nutrition for Rapid Fat Loss

The Best Foods for Burning Stomach Fat

When it comes to burning stomach fat, the key is to focus on consuming foods that will boost your metabolism and help your body burn fat more efficiently. In this subchapter, we will discuss some of the best foods for burning stomach fat and achieving rapid fat loss.

One of the top foods for burning stomach fat is lean protein. Protein is essential for building and repairing muscle, and muscle burns more calories at rest than fat. Some excellent sources of lean protein include chicken, turkey, fish, and tofu. Incorporating protein into every meal can help keep you feeling full and satisfied while also boosting your metabolism.

Another great food for burning stomach fat is leafy greens. Vegetables like spinach, kale, and broccoli are high in fiber and low in calories, making them a great option for those looking to shed unwanted belly fat. Fiber helps to keep you feeling full and aids in digestion, which can help prevent bloating and constipation.

Healthy fats are also essential for burning stomach fat. Foods like avocados, nuts, and olive oil contain unsaturated fats that can help reduce inflammation and boost your metabolism. These fats are also important for hormone production and can help regulate your appetite, making it easier to stick to a healthy eating plan.

In addition to incorporating these foods into your diet, it's important to stay hydrated and limit your consumption of sugary drinks and processed foods. Drinking plenty of water can help flush out toxins and keep your metabolism running smoothly. Avoiding sugary drinks and snacks can help prevent spikes in blood sugar levels, which can lead to increased fat storage in the abdominal area.

By incorporating these foods into your diet and making healthy lifestyle choices, you can effectively burn stomach fat and achieve rapid fat loss. Remember to combine a balanced diet with regular exercise for the best results. With dedication and perseverance, you can reach your weight loss goals and achieve a slimmer, healthier body.

Meal Planning for Quick Results

Meal planning is a crucial component of any successful weight loss journey, especially when it comes to targeting stubborn stomach fat. For people that need to lose stomach fat fast, following a well-thought-out meal plan can make all the difference in achieving quick and sustainable results. In this subchapter, we will discuss some key strategies for meal planning that can help you shed those extra pounds around your midsection in no time.

When it comes to meal planning for quick results, it's important to focus on incorporating nutrient-dense foods that will keep you feeling full and satisfied while also supporting your fat loss goals. This means emphasizing lean proteins, whole grains, fruits, and vegetables while minimizing processed and high-calorie foods. By choosing foods that are high in fiber and protein, you can help regulate your appetite and prevent overeating, which is essential for losing stomach fat quickly.

Another important aspect of meal planning for quick results is portion control. Even healthy foods can contribute to weight gain if consumed in excess, so it's important to pay attention to serving sizes and avoid mindless eating. By measuring out your portions and being mindful of your hunger cues, you can prevent unnecessary calorie intake and accelerate your progress towards a slimmer waistline.

In addition to choosing the right foods and controlling your portions, timing your meals strategically can also play a role in accelerating fat loss. Eating smaller, balanced meals every 3-4 hours can help keep your metabolism revved up and prevent dips in energy levels, which can lead to cravings and overeating. By planning ahead and having healthy snacks on hand, you can avoid reaching for unhealthy options when hunger strikes and stay on track with your weight loss goals.

Overall, meal planning for quick results is all about making smart choices that support your fat loss efforts while keeping you satisfied and energized. By focusing on nutrient-dense foods, controlling your portions, and timing your meals effectively, you can create a meal plan that promotes rapid fat loss and helps you achieve the flat stomach you've been dreaming of. With dedication and consistency, you can see significant results in a short amount of time and finally say goodbye to stubborn stomach fat for good.

Avoiding Common Diet Mistakes

When it comes to losing stomach fat quickly, avoiding common diet mistakes is crucial. Many people make the mistake of drastically cutting their calorie intake in an effort to lose weight fast. While this may lead to initial weight loss, it can actually slow down your metabolism and make it harder to burn fat in the long run. Instead of severely restricting your calories, focus on eating nutrient-dense foods that will fuel your body and help you burn fat more efficiently.

Another common diet mistake that people make when trying to lose stomach fat quickly is relying too heavily on processed foods. These foods are often high in sugar, unhealthy fats, and empty calories, which can sabotage your weight loss efforts. Instead, focus on whole, unprocessed foods like fruits, vegetables, lean proteins, and whole grains. These foods will not only help you lose stomach fat faster, but they will also provide your body with the nutrients it needs to function optimally.

Many people also make the mistake of not drinking enough water when trying to lose stomach fat quickly. Staying hydrated is essential for proper digestion, metabolism, and fat burning. Aim to drink at least eight glasses of water a day, and more if you are exercising or living in a hot climate. Not only will staying hydrated help you lose stomach fat faster, but it will also help you feel more energized and focused throughout the day.

Another common diet mistake that can hinder your efforts to lose stomach fat quickly is skipping meals. Many people believe that skipping meals will help them cut calories and lose weight faster, but this can actually backfire. When you skip meals, your metabolism slows down and your body goes into starvation mode, which can make it harder to burn fat. Instead of skipping meals, aim to eat small, balanced meals throughout the day to keep your metabolism revved up and your energy levels stable.

Finally, one of the biggest diet mistakes people make when trying to lose stomach fat quickly is not getting enough sleep. Sleep is essential for proper hormone balance, metabolism, and fat burning. Aim to get at least seven to eight hours of quality sleep each night to support your weight loss efforts. By avoiding these common diet mistakes and focusing on eating nutrient-dense foods, staying hydrated, eating regular meals, and getting enough sleep, you can maximize your efforts to lose stomach fat quickly and achieve your weight loss goals.

Chapter 4: Exercise Strategies for Shredding Stomach Fat

Cardio Workouts for Maximum Fat Burn

Cardio workouts are an essential component of any weight loss journey, especially when it comes to targeting stubborn stomach fat. These high-intensity exercises are designed to get your heart rate up and increase your calorie burn, making them incredibly effective for shedding fat quickly. In this chapter, we will explore some of the best cardio workouts for maximum fat burn, specifically focusing on techniques that target the abdomen area.

One of the most effective cardio workouts for burning stomach fat is high-intensity interval training (HIIT). This type of workout involves short bursts of intense exercise followed by brief periods of rest or lower-intensity exercise. HIIT has been shown to be incredibly effective at burning calories and increasing metabolism, making it an ideal choice for those looking to lose weight quickly. Incorporating exercises like burpees, mountain climbers, and sprints into your routine can help you achieve maximum fat burn in a short amount of time.

Another great cardio workout for targeting stomach fat is running or jogging. Running is a high-impact exercise that engages multiple muscle groups, including those in the abdomen. By incorporating hills or intervals into your run, you can increase the intensity and challenge your body to burn more calories. Running is also a great way to improve cardiovascular health and endurance, making it a valuable addition to any weight loss program.

Cycling is another effective cardio workout that can help you burn fat and lose weight quickly. Whether you prefer outdoor cycling or using a stationary bike, this low-impact exercise is easy on the joints while still providing a great workout for the legs, core, and cardiovascular system. By varying your speed and resistance levels, you can create a challenging workout that targets stomach fat and improves overall fitness.

In conclusion, incorporating cardio workouts into your routine is essential for maximizing fat burn and achieving rapid weight loss, especially when targeting stubborn stomach fat. Whether you choose HIIT, running, cycling, or another form of cardio exercise, the key is to push yourself to work at a high intensity and challenge your body to burn more calories. By combining these workouts with a healthy diet and consistent exercise routine, you can achieve your weight loss goals and shed stomach fat fast.

Strength Training for a Toned Stomach

If you are looking to achieve a toned stomach and shed excess fat quickly, incorporating strength training into your fitness routine is essential. Strength training not only helps to build muscle and increase metabolism, but it also plays a crucial role in targeting stubborn belly fat. By focusing on specific exercises that engage the core muscles, you can sculpt a lean and defined stomach in no time.

One of the most effective strength training exercises for toning the stomach is the plank. This exercise engages the entire core, including the abdominal muscles, obliques, and lower back. To perform a plank, simply get into a push-up position with your elbows directly beneath your shoulders and hold the position for as long as you can. Aim to gradually increase your hold time as you build strength in your core muscles.

Another effective exercise for toning the stomach is the Russian twist. This exercise targets the obliques and helps to define the waistline. To perform a Russian twist, sit on the floor with your knees bent and feet flat on the ground. Lean back slightly, engage your core, and rotate your torso from side to side, touching the floor beside you with each twist. Aim to complete 3 sets of 15-20 reps on each side.

In addition to targeted core exercises, incorporating compound movements such as squats, deadlifts, and lunges into your strength training routine can help to burn calories and build muscle throughout the entire body. These exercises engage multiple muscle groups at once, leading to greater calorie burn and overall fat loss. Aim to include at least 2-3 compound exercises in each strength training session to maximize results.

Remember, consistency is key when it comes to achieving a toned stomach through strength training. Aim to strength train at least 3-4 times per week, focusing on a variety of exercises that target the core muscles from different angles. Pair your strength training routine with a balanced diet and regular cardiovascular exercise for optimal fat loss results. With dedication and hard work, you can achieve a toned and sculpted stomach in no time.

Incorporating HIIT for Rapid Results

High-Intensity Interval Training (HIIT) has been proven to be one of the most effective methods for burning fat and losing weight quickly. For people that need to lose stomach fat fast, incorporating HIIT into your workout routine is essential. HIIT involves short bursts of intense exercise followed by brief periods of rest, making it a highly efficient way to burn calories and boost metabolism.

One of the key benefits of HIIT is its ability to continue burning calories even after the workout is over. This is known as the afterburn effect, where your body continues to burn calories at a higher rate for hours post-exercise. This makes HIIT a powerful tool for accelerating fat loss and achieving rapid results.

To incorporate HIIT into your routine, start by choosing a few high-intensity exercises that target the core muscles, such as burpees, mountain climbers, and high knees. Perform each exercise at maximum intensity for 20-30 seconds, followed by 10-15 seconds of rest. Repeat this circuit for 15-20 minutes, aiming to push yourself to your limits during each interval.

In addition to its fat-burning benefits, HIIT is also a time-efficient workout option for busy individuals. With HIIT, you can achieve the same results in a fraction of the time compared to traditional steady-state cardio workouts. This makes it ideal for those looking to maximize their fat loss efforts while juggling a hectic schedule.

In conclusion, incorporating HIIT into your workout routine is a highly effective strategy for burning stomach fat fast. By pushing yourself to the limit during short bursts of intense exercise, you can boost your metabolism, burn calories, and achieve rapid results. Whether you're a beginner or an experienced fitness enthusiast, HIIT is a versatile and efficient workout option that can help you reach your fat loss goals in no time.

Chapter 5: Lifestyle Changes for Sustainable Fat Loss

Managing Stress for Weight Loss Success

Managing stress is a crucial component of achieving weight loss success, especially when it comes to targeting stubborn stomach fat. Stress can lead to increased levels of cortisol, a hormone that promotes fat storage in the abdominal area. By implementing stress management techniques such as mindfulness, deep breathing exercises, and regular physical activity, individuals can reduce cortisol levels and create a more conducive environment for fat loss.

One effective stress management technique for weight loss success is practicing mindfulness. Mindfulness involves being fully present in the moment and paying attention to one's thoughts, feelings, and sensations without judgment. By practicing mindfulness regularly, individuals can become more aware of their stress triggers and develop healthier coping mechanisms to avoid emotional eating and other stress-related behaviors that hinder weight loss progress.

Deep breathing exercises are another powerful tool for managing stress and promoting weight loss. When individuals are stressed, their breathing tends to become shallow and rapid, which can further exacerbate feelings of anxiety and tension. By practicing deep breathing exercises, such as diaphragmatic breathing or progressive muscle relaxation, individuals can activate the body's relaxation response and reduce cortisol levels, ultimately supporting their weight loss efforts.

Regular physical activity is also essential for managing stress and achieving weight loss success. Exercise has been shown to reduce stress hormones, such as cortisol, while simultaneously releasing endorphins, which are natural mood boosters. By incorporating a mix of cardiovascular exercise, strength training, and flexibility exercises into their routine, individuals can not only burn calories and build lean muscle mass but also improve their mental well-being and resilience to stress.

In conclusion, managing stress is a critical component of achieving rapid fat loss and shedding stubborn stomach fat. By incorporating stress management techniques such as mindfulness, deep breathing exercises, and regular physical activity into their daily routine, individuals can reduce cortisol levels, improve their emotional well-being, and create a more conducive environment for weight loss success. By addressing both the physical and emotional aspects of weight loss, individuals can achieve sustainable results and enjoy a healthier, happier lifestyle.

Getting Quality Sleep for Fat Loss

Getting quality sleep is crucial for anyone looking to lose stomach fat quickly. Lack of sleep can disrupt hormones that regulate hunger and appetite, leading to increased cravings for unhealthy foods. Inadequate sleep can also slow down metabolism and make it harder for the body to burn fat efficiently. To maximize fat loss, aim for 7-9 hours of quality sleep each night.

One way to improve sleep quality is to establish a consistent bedtime routine. This could include activities such as reading, taking a warm bath, or practicing relaxation techniques like deep breathing or meditation. Creating a relaxing environment in the bedroom, with dim lighting and a comfortable mattress and pillows, can also help promote better sleep.

Avoiding caffeine and electronic devices close to bedtime can also improve sleep quality. Caffeine can interfere with the body's natural sleep-wake cycle, making it harder to fall asleep and stay asleep. Similarly, the blue light emitted by electronic devices can disrupt the production of melatonin, a hormone that regulates sleep. Try to limit caffeine intake and screen time at least an hour before bed for better sleep quality.

Regular exercise can also help improve sleep quality and promote fat loss. Physical activity can help reduce stress and anxiety, two common factors that can interfere with sleep. Additionally, exercise can increase the production of endorphins, chemicals in the brain that promote relaxation and improve mood. Aim for at least 30 minutes of moderate to vigorous exercise most days of the week for optimal sleep and fat loss benefits.

In conclusion, getting quality sleep is essential for anyone looking to lose stomach fat quickly. By establishing a consistent bedtime routine, avoiding caffeine and electronic devices close to bedtime, and incorporating regular exercise into your routine, you can improve sleep quality and maximize fat loss. Prioritizing sleep as part of your fat loss journey can help you achieve your goals more efficiently and effectively.

Tips for Staying Motivated on Your Fat Loss Journey

Losing stomach fat can be a challenging journey, but staying motivated is key to achieving your goals. Here are some tips to help you stay on track and keep your motivation high throughout your fat loss journey.

First and foremost, set realistic and achievable goals for yourself. It's important to have a clear picture of what you want to achieve and how you're going to get there. Break your overall goal into smaller, more manageable milestones that you can track and celebrate along the way. This will help you stay focused and motivated as you see progress being made.

It's also important to find a workout routine that you enjoy and that fits into your schedule. Whether it's hitting the gym, going for a run, or trying out a new workout class, finding activities that you look forward to will make it easier to stay consistent and motivated. Remember, exercise doesn't have to be boring or monotonous – find something that you love and stick with it.

In addition to finding a workout routine that you enjoy, make sure to also focus on your nutrition. Eating a balanced diet filled with whole, nutrient-dense foods will not only help you lose stomach fat faster, but it will also give you the energy you need to power through your workouts. Stay hydrated, limit processed foods, and make sure you're getting enough protein, healthy fats, and fiber in your diet.

Lastly, surround yourself with a supportive community. Whether it's joining a fitness class, finding a workout buddy, or following motivational accounts on social media, having a support system can make all the difference in staying motivated on your fat loss journey. Share your progress, celebrate your wins, and lean on others for encouragement when you need it. Remember, you're not alone in this journey – there are plenty of others out there going through the same struggles and triumphs as you.

Chapter 6: Supplementing Your Fat Loss Efforts

The Best Fat-Burning Supplements

In the quest to shed stubborn stomach fat quickly and efficiently, many people turn to fat-burning supplements to give them an extra edge. With a plethora of options available on the market, it can be overwhelming to navigate through the abundance of products claiming to aid in fat loss. However, there are a few key supplements that have been proven to be effective in accelerating the fat-burning process.

One of the most popular fat-burning supplements is green tea extract. Green tea contains catechins, a type of antioxidant that has been shown to increase metabolism and promote fat oxidation. By incorporating green tea extract into your daily routine, you can boost your body's ability to burn fat, especially in the abdominal area where stubborn fat tends to accumulate.

Another powerful fat-burning supplement is caffeine. Caffeine is a stimulant that can increase energy levels and enhance focus, making it easier to stay active and motivated during workouts. Additionally, caffeine has been found to boost metabolism and promote the breakdown of fat cells, making it an effective tool for those looking to trim their waistline.

Yohimbine is another popular fat-burning supplement that has gained traction in the fitness community. Yohimbine works by blocking receptors in the body that inhibit fat loss, allowing for greater mobilization of stored fat. This can be especially beneficial for those struggling to lose stomach fat, as yohimbine targets stubborn areas where fat tends to linger.

In addition to these supplements, many people also turn to conjugated linoleic acid (CLA) to aid in fat loss. CLA is a fatty acid that has been shown to reduce body fat levels, particularly in the abdominal region. By incorporating CLA into your supplement regimen, you can support your body's ability to burn fat and achieve a leaner, more toned physique.

When it comes to selecting the best fat-burning supplements for your needs, it's important to do your research and consult with a healthcare professional before starting any new regimen. By incorporating these key supplements into your routine, you can accelerate your fat loss journey and achieve the toned stomach you've been working towards. Remember, supplements are just one piece of the puzzle – be sure to also focus on a balanced diet and regular exercise to maximize your results.

Understanding the Role of Supplements in Fat Loss

When it comes to shedding stubborn stomach fat quickly, many people turn to supplements to help accelerate their weight loss journey. While supplements can be a helpful tool in achieving your fat loss goals, it's important to understand their role and how they can aid in your overall success.

One of the most popular types of supplements for fat loss is thermogenics. These supplements work by increasing your body's core temperature, which in turn helps to boost your metabolism and burn more calories throughout the day. This can be especially beneficial for those looking to lose stomach fat fast, as a faster metabolism means more efficient fat burning.

Another key supplement in the fat loss world is protein powder. Protein is essential for building and repairing muscle tissue, and having an adequate intake can help to preserve muscle mass while you're in a calorie deficit. This is important for fat loss, as muscle tissue plays a crucial role in maintaining a healthy metabolism. Protein powder can also help to keep you feeling full and satisfied, making it easier to stick to your diet and avoid overeating.

In addition to thermogenics and protein powder, there are a variety of other supplements that can aid in fat loss. These include fat burners, which help to increase the breakdown of fat cells, as well as appetite suppressants, which can help to control cravings and reduce overall calorie intake. It's important to note that while supplements can be helpful, they should not be relied upon as a sole means of achieving fat loss. A balanced diet and regular exercise are still essential components of any successful fat loss plan.

Ultimately, the role of supplements in fat loss is to support your overall efforts and help you reach your goals more quickly. By incorporating the right supplements into your routine and combining them with a healthy diet and regular exercise, you can maximize your results and achieve the lean, toned stomach you desire. Remember to consult with a healthcare professional before starting any new supplement regimen to ensure it is safe and appropriate for your individual needs.

Avoiding Scams and Gimmicks in the Supplement Industry

In the quest to lose stomach fat quickly, many people turn to supplements as a way to accelerate their weight loss journey. However, the supplement industry is rife with scams and gimmicks that can not only waste your money but also potentially harm your health. It is crucial to be vigilant and informed when navigating this market to ensure you are not falling victim to false promises and deceptive marketing tactics.

One of the most common scams in the supplement industry is the promise of "miraculous" weight loss results with little to no effort on your part. Beware of products that claim you can shed pounds overnight or without making any changes to your diet and exercise routine. Sustainable weight loss requires a combination of healthy eating, regular physical activity, and consistency – there are no shortcuts or magic pills that can replace these fundamental principles.

Another red flag to watch out for is supplements that make exaggerated claims or use flashy marketing techniques to lure you in. If a product sounds too good to be true, it probably is. Look for supplements that have scientific evidence backing their efficacy and are recommended by reputable health professionals. Do your research, read reviews from trusted sources, and consult with a healthcare provider before adding any new supplement to your regimen.

It is also important to be wary of supplements that contain hidden or unlisted ingredients, as these can pose serious risks to your health. Always read the label carefully and choose products that are transparent about their ingredients and manufacturing processes. Avoid products that use proprietary blends or have vague labeling – you have the right to know exactly what you are putting into your body.

In conclusion, when it comes to navigating the supplement industry in your quest to lose stomach fat fast, it is essential to be discerning and cautious. Avoid falling for scams and gimmicks by doing your due diligence, seeking out reputable products, and consulting with healthcare professionals. Remember that sustainable weight loss requires a holistic approach that includes healthy eating, regular exercise, and patience – there are no quick fixes or shortcuts that can replace these foundational principles. By staying informed and making educated choices, you can safely and effectively support your fat loss goals with the help of supplements.

Chapter 7: Maintaining Your Fat Loss Results

Creating a Sustainable Maintenance Plan

Creating a sustainable maintenance plan is essential for long-term success when it comes to losing stomach fat quickly. It's not enough to just shed the pounds - you need to maintain your results to prevent regaining the weight. This subchapter will provide you with tips and strategies to help you create a sustainable maintenance plan that will keep you on track and help you achieve your weight loss goals.

One of the most important aspects of creating a sustainable maintenance plan is to focus on making small, gradual changes to your lifestyle. This could include incorporating more physical activity into your daily routine, such as going for a walk after dinner or taking the stairs instead of the elevator. By making small changes over time, you can create habits that will help you maintain your weight loss results in the long run.

Another key component of a sustainable maintenance plan is to focus on eating a balanced and nutritious diet. This means incorporating plenty of fruits, vegetables, whole grains, and lean proteins into your meals while limiting processed foods and sugary drinks. By fueling your body with nutrient-dense foods, you can support your weight loss efforts and maintain your results over time.

In addition to diet and exercise, it's important to prioritize self-care and stress management as part of your maintenance plan. Chronic stress can contribute to weight gain and make it harder to lose stomach fat, so finding healthy ways to manage stress is crucial. This could include practicing mindfulness, meditation, yoga, or engaging in hobbies that bring you joy and relaxation.

Finally, accountability and support are key components of a sustainable maintenance plan. Surround yourself with friends, family, or a support group who can cheer you on and hold you accountable to your goals. By staying connected to others who are on a similar journey, you can stay motivated and inspired to continue making healthy choices and maintaining your weight loss results for the long term.

Dealing with Setbacks and Plateaus

Dealing with setbacks and plateaus is a common challenge when trying to lose stomach fat quickly. It's important to remember that setbacks are a natural part of the weight loss journey and should not be seen as failures. Instead, they should be viewed as opportunities to learn and grow. Plateaus, on the other hand, can be frustrating, but they are also a normal part of the process. Understanding how to navigate these obstacles is crucial to achieving your weight loss goals.

When faced with a setback, it's important to stay positive and not get discouraged. Remember that setbacks are temporary and can be overcome with dedication and perseverance. Take a moment to reflect on what may have caused the setback and make a plan to avoid similar situations in the future. Whether it's a slip-up in your diet or a missed workout, use setbacks as a learning experience to help you stay on track towards your goals.

Plateaus are a common occurrence when trying to lose weight quickly, especially when it comes to losing stubborn stomach fat. The key to overcoming plateaus is to mix up your routine and make small changes to keep your body guessing. This can include trying new workouts, increasing the intensity of your current workouts, or adjusting your diet. By keeping your body challenged, you can break through plateaus and continue making progress towards your weight loss goals.

In addition to making changes to your routine, it's also important to stay patient and consistent. Weight loss is not always linear, and there will be times when progress slows down or stalls. It's important to trust the process and continue putting in the work, even when results are not immediate. Remember that slow progress is still progress, and every small step forward brings you closer to your ultimate goal of shedding stomach fat fast.

Overall, setbacks and plateaus are a normal part of the weight loss journey, especially when trying to lose stomach fat quickly. By staying positive, learning from setbacks, and making small changes to overcome plateaus, you can stay on track towards achieving your goals. Remember to be patient, consistent, and dedicated to your weight loss journey, and you will eventually see the results you desire.

Celebrating Your Successes and Setting New Goals

Congratulations on taking the first steps towards achieving your weight loss goals! It's important to celebrate your successes, no matter how small they may seem. Whether you've lost a few pounds or have been sticking to a healthier diet, it's essential to acknowledge your progress and give yourself a pat on the back. Remember, every step forward is a step closer to your ultimate goal of shredding stomach fat.

As you celebrate your successes, it's also crucial to set new goals to keep yourself motivated and on track. Setting specific, measurable, achievable, relevant, and time-bound (SMART) goals can help you stay focused and accountable. Whether you want to lose a certain number of inches from your waist or fit into a specific pair of jeans, having clear goals in mind will help you stay committed to your weight loss journey.

When setting new goals, it's important to be realistic and to break them down into smaller, more manageable steps. For example, if your ultimate goal is to lose 20 pounds of stomach fat, set smaller goals such as losing 5 pounds in the first month. By achieving these smaller goals, you'll build confidence and momentum to keep pushing forward towards your larger goal.

In addition to celebrating your successes and setting new goals, it's essential to track your progress along the way. Keeping a food journal, logging your workouts, and taking measurements of your waistline can help you stay accountable and see how far you've come. Tracking your progress can also help you identify any areas where you may need to make adjustments to your diet or exercise routine.

Remember, losing stomach fat is a journey, not a destination. By celebrating your successes, setting new goals, and tracking your progress, you'll stay motivated and committed to achieving your ultimate goal of rapid fat loss. Keep pushing yourself, stay focused, and never give up on your weight loss goals. You've got this!

Recipes

Breakfast

Avocado Toast with Poached Eggs

- 1 slice whole-grain bread
- 1/2 avocado, mashed
- 1 poached egg
- Salt, pepper, and red pepper flakes to taste
- Fresh lemon juice

Instructions:

1. Toast the bread.
2. Spread mashed avocado on the toast.
3. Top with a poached egg.
4. Season with salt, pepper, red pepper flakes, and a squeeze of lemon juice.

Snack

Greek Yogurt with Berries

- 1 cup Greek yogurt
- 1/2 cup mixed berries (blueberries, raspberries, strawberries)
- 1 tablespoon chia seeds or flaxseeds
- Drizzle of honey (optional)

Instructions:

1. Combine Greek yogurt and berries in a bowl.
2. Sprinkle with chia seeds or flaxseeds.
3. Add a drizzle of honey if desired.

Lunch

Quinoa Salad with Grilled Chicken

- 1 cup cooked quinoa
- 1 grilled chicken breast, sliced
- 1 cup mixed greens (spinach, arugula, kale)
- 1/2 cup cherry tomatoes, halved
- 1/4 cup diced cucumber
- 1/4 cup feta cheese
- 2 tablespoons olive oil

- 1 tablespoon balsamic vinegar
- Salt and pepper to taste

Instructions:

1. In a large bowl, mix quinoa, mixed greens, cherry tomatoes, cucumber, and feta cheese.
2. Top with grilled chicken slices.
3. Drizzle with olive oil and balsamic vinegar.
4. Season with salt and pepper.

Dinner

Salmon with Asparagus

- 1 salmon fillet
- 1 bunch of asparagus, trimmed
- 1 tablespoon olive oil
- 1 lemon, sliced
- Salt and pepper to taste
- Fresh dill or parsley for garnish

Instructions:

1. Preheat oven to 400°F (200°C).
2. Place salmon fillet and asparagus on a baking sheet.
3. Drizzle with olive oil and season with salt and pepper.
4. Lay lemon slices on top of the salmon.
5. Bake for 15-20 minutes, until the salmon is cooked through.
6. Garnish with fresh dill or parsley.

Evening Snack

Apple Slices with Almond Butter

- 1 apple, sliced
- 2 tablespoons almond butter

Instructions:

1. Slice the apple.
2. Dip slices into almond butter.

Tips for Reducing Belly Fat:

1. **Stay Hydrated:** Drink plenty of water throughout the day.

2. **Avoid Sugary Drinks:** Replace sodas and sugary drinks with water, herbal teas, or infused water.
3. **Eat Plenty of Fiber:** Incorporate foods high in soluble fiber, such as oats, flaxseeds, avocados, and legumes.
4. **Get Enough Sleep:** Aim for 7-9 hours of quality sleep per night.
5. **Exercise Regularly:** Combine cardio workouts with strength training exercises.
6. **Reduce Stress:** Practice mindfulness, yoga, or meditation to manage stress levels.

Breakfast

Overnight Chia Pudding

- 1/4 cup chia seeds
- 1 cup unsweetened almond milk
- 1 teaspoon vanilla extract
- 1 tablespoon maple syrup or honey (optional)
- Fresh berries for topping

Instructions:

1. In a jar, combine chia seeds, almond milk, vanilla extract, and sweetener (if using).
2. Stir well and refrigerate overnight.
3. In the morning, top with fresh berries before serving.

Snack

Veggie Sticks with Hummus

- 1 cup sliced veggies (carrots, celery, bell peppers, cucumber)
- 1/4 cup hummus

Instructions:

1. Slice the veggies into sticks.
2. Serve with hummus for dipping.

Lunch

Turkey and Avocado Lettuce Wraps

- 4 large lettuce leaves (romaine or butter lettuce)
- 8 slices of turkey breast
- 1 avocado, sliced

- 1/2 red bell pepper, sliced
- 1/4 red onion, thinly sliced
- Mustard or your favorite sauce

Instructions:

1. Lay the lettuce leaves flat.
2. Place turkey slices, avocado, bell pepper, and onion on each leaf.
3. Drizzle with mustard or your favorite sauce.
4. Wrap the lettuce around the fillings and serve.

Dinner

Spaghetti Squash with Tomato and Basil

- 1 spaghetti squash
- 2 tablespoons olive oil
- 2 cloves garlic, minced
- 2 cups cherry tomatoes, halved
- Salt and pepper to taste
- Fresh basil leaves, chopped
- Grated Parmesan cheese (optional)

Instructions:

1. Preheat the oven to 400°F (200°C).
2. Cut the spaghetti squash in half lengthwise and scoop out the seeds.
3. Drizzle the insides with 1 tablespoon olive oil, and season with salt and pepper.
4. Place the squash cut-side down on a baking sheet and roast for 40 minutes.
5. While the squash is roasting, heat the remaining olive oil in a skillet over medium heat.
6. Add garlic and cherry tomatoes, cooking until tomatoes are soft.
7. Remove the squash from the oven, scrape the insides with a fork to create spaghetti-like strands, and add them to the skillet.
8. Toss with tomatoes and garlic, season with salt and pepper, and top with fresh basil and Parmesan cheese if desired.

Evening Snack

Green Smoothie

- 1 cup spinach
- 1/2 banana
- 1/2 cup frozen mango
- 1 tablespoon chia seeds
- 1 cup unsweetened almond milk

Instructions:

1. Blend all ingredients until smooth.
2. Pour into a glass and enjoy.

Additional Tips:

1. **Limit Refined Carbs:** Avoid white bread, pasta, and sugary snacks.
2. **Eat Healthy Fats:** Include sources like avocados, nuts, seeds, and olive oil.
3. **Increase Protein Intake:** Helps with satiety and muscle maintenance. Good sources include lean meats, fish, eggs, and legumes.
4. **Stay Active:** Incorporate daily physical activities, such as walking, cycling, or swimming, along with regular workouts.
5. **Mindful Eating:** Pay attention to hunger and fullness cues, and avoid eating out of boredom or stress.

Breakfast

Spinach and Mushroom Egg White Omelette

- 3 egg whites
- 1 cup fresh spinach
- 1/2 cup sliced mushrooms
- 1/4 cup diced tomatoes
- 1 tablespoon olive oil
- Salt and pepper to taste

Instructions:

1. Heat olive oil in a non-stick skillet over medium heat.
2. Add mushrooms and sauté until tender.
3. Add spinach and cook until wilted.
4. Pour egg whites over the vegetables and cook until set.
5. Season with salt and pepper, and top with diced tomatoes before serving.

Snack

Cucumber and Hummus Bites

- 1 cucumber, sliced into rounds
- 1/4 cup hummus
- Paprika and chopped parsley for garnish

Instructions:

1. Spread a small dollop of hummus on each cucumber slice.
2. Sprinkle with paprika and chopped parsley.

Lunch

Tuna and White Bean Salad

- 1 can of tuna in water, drained
- 1 can of white beans, rinsed and drained
- 1/2 red onion, finely chopped
- 1/2 cup cherry tomatoes, halved
- 1/4 cup chopped parsley
- 2 tablespoons olive oil
- 1 tablespoon lemon juice
- Salt and pepper to taste

Instructions:

1. In a large bowl, combine tuna, white beans, red onion, cherry tomatoes, and parsley.
2. Drizzle with olive oil and lemon juice.
3. Season with salt and pepper, and toss to combine.

Dinner

Chicken and Vegetable Stir-Fry

- 1 boneless, skinless chicken breast, thinly sliced
- 1 red bell pepper, sliced
- 1 cup broccoli florets
- 1 carrot, julienned
- 2 tablespoons soy sauce (or tamari for gluten-free)
- 1 tablespoon sesame oil
- 1 tablespoon grated ginger
- 2 cloves garlic, minced
- 1 tablespoon sesame seeds (optional)

Instructions:

1. Heat sesame oil in a large skillet or wok over medium-high heat.
2. Add chicken slices and cook until no longer pink.
3. Add garlic and ginger, and sauté for 1 minute.
4. Add bell pepper, broccoli, and carrot, and stir-fry until vegetables are tender-crisp.
5. Stir in soy sauce and cook for another 2 minutes.
6. Sprinkle with sesame seeds before serving.

Berry and Nut Mix

- 1/4 cup mixed berries (blueberries, raspberries, strawberries)
- 2 tablespoons mixed nuts (almonds, walnuts, cashews)

Instructions:

1. Combine berries and nuts in a bowl.
2. Enjoy as a healthy, nutrient-packed snack.

Additional Tips:

1. **Stay Consistent:** Consistency is key in any weight loss journey. Stick to your healthy eating and exercise routine.
2. **Portion Control:** Be mindful of portion sizes to avoid overeating, even healthy foods.
3. **Stay Hydrated:** Drinking water before meals can help control appetite and prevent overeating.
4. **Limit Alcohol:** Alcohol can add unnecessary calories and hinder weight loss efforts.
5. **Incorporate HIIT:** High-intensity interval training (HIIT) can be very effective for burning belly fat.

Breakfast

Greek Yogurt Parfait

- 1 cup Greek yogurt
- 1/2 cup granola (preferably low-sugar)
- 1/2 cup mixed berries (strawberries, blueberries, raspberries)
- 1 tablespoon honey
- 1 tablespoon chia seeds

Instructions:

1. In a glass or bowl, layer Greek yogurt, granola, and mixed berries.
2. Drizzle with honey.
3. Sprinkle chia seeds on top before serving.

Snack

Apple Slices with Peanut Butter

- 1 apple, sliced
- 2 tablespoons natural peanut butter

Instructions:

1. Slice the apple into wedges.
2. Spread peanut butter on each slice.

Lunch

Grilled Chicken Salad with Avocado

- 1 grilled chicken breast, sliced
- 4 cups mixed greens (spinach, arugula, kale)
- 1/2 avocado, sliced
- 1/2 cup cherry tomatoes, halved
- 1/4 cup red onion, thinly sliced
- 2 tablespoons olive oil
- 1 tablespoon balsamic vinegar
- Salt and pepper to taste

Instructions:

1. In a large bowl, combine mixed greens, cherry tomatoes, and red onion.
2. Top with grilled chicken slices and avocado.
3. Drizzle with olive oil and balsamic vinegar.
4. Season with salt and pepper.

Dinner

Baked Cod with Lemon and Dill

- 2 cod fillets
- 2 tablespoons olive oil
- 1 lemon, sliced
- 1 tablespoon fresh dill, chopped
- Salt and pepper to taste

Instructions:

1. Preheat oven to 400°F (200°C).
2. Place cod fillets in a baking dish.
3. Drizzle with olive oil and season with salt and pepper.
4. Lay lemon slices on top of the fillets.
5. Sprinkle with fresh dill.
6. Bake for 15-20 minutes, or until the fish is opaque and flakes easily with a fork.

Kale Chips

- 1 bunch of kale, stems removed and leaves torn into bite-sized pieces
- 1 tablespoon olive oil
- Salt to taste

Instructions:

1. Preheat oven to 350°F (175°C).
2. Toss kale with olive oil and salt.
3. Spread kale on a baking sheet in a single layer.
4. Bake for 10-15 minutes, or until crispy.

Additional Tips:

1. **Avoid Processed Foods:** Stick to whole, unprocessed foods as much as possible.
2. **Eat More Protein:** Protein helps with satiety and muscle maintenance. Include sources like lean meats, fish, eggs, and legumes.
3. **Reduce Sugar Intake:** Minimize added sugars in your diet by avoiding sugary drinks, sweets, and processed foods.
4. **Get Moving:** Incorporate regular physical activity into your routine. Both cardio and strength training exercises are beneficial.
5. **Manage Stress:** Chronic stress can lead to weight gain, especially around the belly. Practice stress-reducing activities like yoga, meditation, or deep breathing exercises.

Breakfast

Oatmeal with Berries and Nuts

- 1/2 cup rolled oats
- 1 cup water or unsweetened almond milk
- 1/2 cup mixed berries (blueberries, strawberries, raspberries)
- 1 tablespoon chopped nuts (almonds, walnuts, pecans)
- 1 teaspoon honey or maple syrup (optional)
- 1/2 teaspoon cinnamon

Instructions:

1. In a pot, bring water or almond milk to a boil.
2. Add rolled oats and reduce heat to a simmer. Cook for about 5 minutes, stirring occasionally.

3. Once the oats are cooked, transfer to a bowl.
4. Top with mixed berries, chopped nuts, and a drizzle of honey or maple syrup if desired.
5. Sprinkle with cinnamon.

Snack

Bell Pepper and Guacamole

- 1 bell pepper, sliced
- 1/2 cup guacamole

Instructions:

1. Slice the bell pepper into strips.
2. Serve with guacamole for dipping.

Lunch

Lentil and Vegetable Soup

- 1 cup dried lentils, rinsed
- 1 tablespoon olive oil
- 1 onion, chopped
- 2 carrots, chopped
- 2 celery stalks, chopped
- 3 cloves garlic, minced
- 1 can (14.5 ounces) diced tomatoes
- 4 cups vegetable broth
- 1 teaspoon cumin
- 1 teaspoon paprika
- Salt and pepper to taste
- Fresh parsley for garnish

Instructions:

1. Heat olive oil in a large pot over medium heat.
2. Add onion, carrots, and celery. Sauté until vegetables are tender, about 5-7 minutes.
3. Add garlic and cook for another minute.
4. Stir in lentils, diced tomatoes, vegetable broth, cumin, and paprika.
5. Bring to a boil, then reduce heat and simmer for 30-40 minutes, or until lentils are tender.
6. Season with salt and pepper.
7. Garnish with fresh parsley before serving.

Stuffed Bell Peppers

- 4 bell peppers, tops cut off and seeds removed
- 1 cup cooked quinoa
- 1/2 pound ground turkey or chicken
- 1 cup black beans, rinsed and drained
- 1 cup corn kernels
- 1 cup diced tomatoes
- 1 teaspoon cumin
- 1 teaspoon chili powder
- Salt and pepper to taste
- 1/2 cup shredded cheese (optional)

Instructions:

1. Preheat oven to 375°F (190°C).
2. In a skillet, cook ground turkey or chicken until browned. Drain any excess fat.
3. In a large bowl, combine cooked quinoa, ground meat, black beans, corn, diced tomatoes, cumin, chili powder, salt, and pepper.
4. Stuff each bell pepper with the mixture and place in a baking dish.
5. If using, sprinkle shredded cheese on top.
6. Cover with foil and bake for 30-35 minutes, or until peppers are tender.
7. Remove foil and bake for an additional 5 minutes to melt the cheese.

Evening Snack

Protein Smoothie

- 1 scoop protein powder (choose a low-sugar option)
- 1 cup unsweetened almond milk
- 1/2 banana
- 1 tablespoon almond butter
- 1/2 teaspoon cinnamon
- Ice cubes (optional)

Instructions:

1. Combine all ingredients in a blender.
2. Blend until smooth.
3. Pour into a glass and enjoy.

1. **Incorporate Healthy Fats:** Include sources of healthy fats like avocados, nuts, seeds, and olive oil in your diet.
2. **Stay Hydrated:** Drink plenty of water throughout the day to help with digestion and metabolism.
3. **Limit Refined Carbs:** Avoid foods like white bread, pasta, and pastries. Choose whole grains instead.
4. **Regular Exercise:** Aim for a combination of cardio and strength training exercises to burn fat and build muscle.
5. **Mindful Eating:** Pay attention to portion sizes and eat slowly to give your body time to signal when it's full.